Consumerism

Critical World Issues

Abortion
Animal Rights
The Arms Trade
Capital Punishment
Consumerism
Drugs
Equal Opportunities
Euthanasia

Food Technology
Genetic Engineering
Genocide
Human Rights
Poverty
Racism
Refugees
Terrorism

CRITICAL WORLD ISSUES

Consumerism

Martin Johnson

MASON CREST
PHILADELPHIA

Mason Crest
450 Parkway Drive, Suite D
Broomall, PA 19008
www.masoncrest.com

©2017 by Mason Crest, an imprint of National Highlights, Inc.

Printed and bound in the United States of America.

CPSIA Compliance Information: Batch #CWI2016.
For further information, contact Mason Crest at 1-866-MCP-Book.

First printing
1 3 5 7 9 8 6 4 2

Library of Congress Cataloging-in-Publication Data

on file at the Library of Congress
ISBN: 978-1-4222-3650-5 (hc)
ISBN: 978-1-4222-8130-7 (ebook)

Critical World Issues series ISBN: 978-1-4222-3645-1

Table of Contents

KEY ICONS TO LOOK FOR:

 Words to Understand: These words with their easy-to-understand definitions will increase the reader's understanding of the text, while building vocabulary skills.

 Sidebars: This boxed material within the main text allows readers to build knowledge, gain insights, explore possibilities, and broaden their perspectives by weaving together additional information to provide realistic and holistic perspectives.

 Research Projects: Readers are pointed toward areas of further inquiry connected to each chapter. Suggestions are provided for projects that encourage deeper research and analysis.

 Text-Dependent Questions: These questions send the reader back to the text for more careful attention to the evidence presented there.

 Series Glossary of Key Terms: This back-of-the book glossary contains terminology used throughout this series. Words found here increase the reader's ability to read and comprehend higher-level books and articles in this field.

1

Introduction to Consumerism

We buy all kinds of products every day, but we rarely stop to think about how those products reached the stores or what hidden costs they might contain. The following story is about someone working in India's carpet industry. The carpets made there are sold to stores in Europe and the United States. One of them may have even ended up on your floor. . . .

Rajendra's Story

Rajendra is 14. He is a carpet weaver in the state of Uttar Pradesh in northeastern India. He works on a loom for 15 hours a day, 7 days a week, with only a short break for lunch. For this, he is paid 10 rupees (22 cents) per day by the loom owner. At noon, he is given two roti (pieces of bread) with salt,

These neon ads in New York City's Times Square reflect the desire of companies to push their products 24 hours a day, even after most people have gone to bed!

and the same again when he ends work in the evening. The loom is in a small, poorly-lit village hut with tiny, heavily-barred windows.

Rajendra has worked here for three years. His father, Bhagwan, was too poor to take care of his large family and went to the loom owner for a loan. In return, Rajendra was forced to work for the loom owner. In the early days, he would make mistakes or would work too slowly, for which the loom owner would beat him with a bamboo stick.

Children are sought after for carpet weaving because their nimble fingers and good eyesight suit the detailed motions required to weave carpets, from 30 to 40 square feet in size, one thread at a time.

Rajendra's eyesight is now poor, he has lung disease from

 Words to Understand in This Chapter

24-hour society—a modern society in which people can buy goods, work, go to restaurants, etc. all night and all day.

aristocracy—the highest social class in a country.

consumer—one who buys goods and services.

consumerism—an attitude that values the purchase of goods that are desirable but not essential.

planned obsolescence—making or designing something (such as a car) in such a way that it will only be usable for a short time, so that people will have to buy another one.

producer—one who provides goods and services.

product placement—the inclusion of a product in a television program or film as a form of paid advertisement.

A craftsman uses a handloom to produce rugs in Jodhpur, India.

inhaling wool particles, and his back is bent from spending such long hours at the loom. Lack of nutritious food has made him small for his age.

Rajendra is just one of thousands of children who weave carpets in India. Most of them live and work in appalling conditions, and yet they are part of a very lucrative industry: Indian carpet exports profit around $600 million per year; half of these carpets are sold in the United States.

Consumerism Defined

People have always had basic needs such as food, clothing, and shelter. As societies grew wealthier, however, people's appetites changed. They became interested in acquiring things for reasons other than mere survival. *Consumerism* is an attitude that values the purchase of goods that are desirable but not essential.

In a consumerist society, people can become caught up in the process of shopping and take part of their identity from the new items they buy. They may be concerned with the clothes, cars, and household furnishings they purchase because these things build an image they wish to project about themselves.

Consumerism is driven by *consumers*, who have a desire for luxury goods, as well as by *producers*, who are looking for profits. On the production side, a number of industries are employed to satisfy consumerism and generate more of it. Researchers develop new products to tempt consumers, designers find fresh ways to make products attractive, ads bring these products and services to the attention of the public, and retailers work to lure customers into their stores.

Main Effects of Consumerism

Consumerism has affected society in many ways—some good, some bad. It has led to a breakdown of traditional social divisions as people of all socioeconomic backgrounds have gained access to a wide range of luxury goods. On the other hand, it has given rise to a greater division between the rich and poor: producers have exploited laborers in poorer countries, who work for less money than those in richer countries, in order to

Companies like Apple, Inc. want consumers who purchase their products to feel like they are hip and fashionable.

In Brazil, the growing worldwide demand for beef has meant the destruction of rainforests to clear land for pastures. This has caused a loss of fertile topsoil and a severe reduction in the water supply, because of the water needed for cattle and to grow their feed.

increase their profits. Consumerism has also taken its toll on the environment with expanding demand leading to an unsustainable use of natural resources.

Modern consumers expect a wider selection of products and services, as well as the freedom to buy them whenever they wish. As a result, the world is fast becoming a *24-hour society*, where goods and services can be purchased at any time of the day or night. Many stores are now open from 7:00 a.m. until

11:00 p.m., and some are open 24 hours a day, seven days a week. Whether over the telephone or Internet, vacations, books, food, banking, and legal services can be purchased at all times, 365 days a year. This allows people to do their shopping at a time that suits them, while producers can sell nonstop. The 24-hour society has also changed the world of work, with more people working longer or more flexible hours rather than the traditional nine-to-five workday.

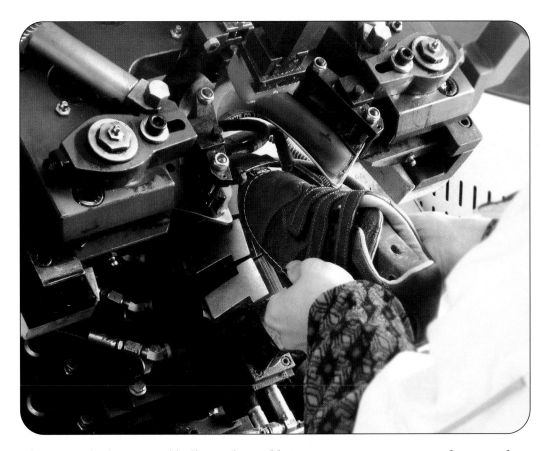

Chinese-made shoes are sold all over the world. However, customers may not be aware that the workers in these Chinese shoe factories are regularly required to work 16 hours a day, seven days a week, and that drops in production can lead to brutal punishments.

Beginnings of Consumerism

Consumerism has its origins in ancient times. In the first century BCE, noble-born Romans acquired a taste for luxury products, such as silk from China. By the 13th century CE, European *aristocracy* had become interested in clothing, goods, and spices from the Far East. Possession of these was often used to display a person's wealth and status—a key aspect of consumerism.

However, unlike today, these early forms of consumerism only affected a small, wealthy minority. Most people in ancient

 ## The Umbrellas

A classic early consumer product, the umbrella, was first used by the Ancient Egyptians and Romans to shelter them from the weather. During the Middle Ages, however, umbrellas were regarded as something of a novelty, and their use declined. In the seventeenth century, Europeans became discontent with getting wet—something that had never bothered them much before. French nobles began using umbrellas, having borrowed the idea from the Chinese, and their usage gradually filtered down through society. Umbrellas reached rainy England in the 1770s, where they were criticized at first for being unmanly and foreign. However, they soon caught on and are now very much a part of English identity.

and medieval societies were too poor to develop consumerist urges. Much of their trade was based on exchanging goods and services rather than buying them with money, so there was little cash available to buy luxury products. There is also evidence to suggest that in medieval times, people were often deterred from acquiring unnecessary products because of their religious beliefs. Christianity and Buddhism, in particular, stressed that worldly possessions made it harder to achieve spiritual salvation.

Consumerism in its modern form first emerged in Western Europe in the late seventeenth century. By this time, a middle class consisting of business people, merchants, and professionals had established itself.

Colonies were being set up in the Americas and the Far East, giving this class of wealthy Europeans access to many exotic products. Early consumer favorites included sugar and coffee from the Americas, tea and porcelain from China, spices from Southeast Asia, and cotton from India.

In the eighteenth century, new ways of advertising and selling goods were developed. Shopkeepers began enticing customers into their stores with window displays or offers of discounts and bargains. Advertisements filled the newspapers that began appearing in cities. Consumers became susceptible to fads and fashions. For example, in the early 1700s, there was a craze for tall hats, wigs, and wide skirts for women. By the end of the century, people became more conscious of body odor, causing a boom in perfume sales for both sexes. The patterns of buying and selling that were established in the eighteenth century continue to this day.

Expansion of Consumerism

The next big development in consumerism came with the arrival of the department store. The first one opened in Paris in the 1830s, and the concept quickly spread to major cities throughout Europe and North America. Consumers were now presented with a vast range of products, attractively displayed, in spacious surroundings. Department stores were visited as much for the pleasure of the experience as for the practical matter of purchasing. Browsing became a popular pastime, and shopping was transformed into a leisure activity. Another 19th-century innovation was the catalog, which allowed rural and small-town dwellers to buy from major stores by ordering

Modern supermarkets carry a variety of products and fresh foods from all over the world.

Some "superstores" have expanded the range of goods they sell beyond just foodstuffs, and today offer clothing, books, banking services, and even cars!

goods that could be sent by mail.

In the early twentieth century, manufacturers of long-lasting consumer products, such as cars, faced the problem that their customers would only buy from them occasionally. They solved this by introducing the *planned obsolescence* of their products. By bringing out a new range of products with better features each year, they could persuade customers that what they bought the previous year was now out of date.

In the twentieth century, technological advances made it possible to create new products, including artificial fabrics like

Product Placement

In the 1982 film *ET*, a candy called Reese's Pieces appeared in an important scene, causing sales of this product to jump by 65 percent. Ever since then, *product placement*—the inclusion of products in movies, TV, and even video games—has become a significant promotional technique. Interactive TV will allow viewers to order a featured product—for example a shirt being worn by a TV star—simply by clicking on it.

Digital advertising uses computer technology to insert products into scenes that were never there to begin with. This is most commonly seen in televised sporting events, where ads are projected onto billboards or playing surfaces in stadiums. The fans in attendance at the event can't see the advertisements, but millions watching the game at home see them clearly on their television screen.

Broadcasters can use digital technology to insert advertisements into the blank space on the wall behind the batter in this baseball game. This way the ads can be changed every inning. Only viewers at home will see them; patrons at the game will only see a blank wall.

nylon, music systems, and computers. New means of advertising and selling were made possible by the emergence of radio in the 1920s, television in the 1950s, and the Internet in the 1990s.

Consumerism also spread to many different activities in the twentieth century. In the 1920s and 1930s, eating out became popular with the opening of fish and chip shops in the United Kingdom (UK) and hamburger restaurants in the United States. Consumerism also affected transportation, first with the invention of the bicycle and, later on, the car. With the development of the airplane, vacations abroad became another major consumer purchase. Today, almost every major field of human activity is affected by consumerism, including religious festivals, weddings, and child rearing.

Shopping has become a popular way for people of all ages to relax and have fun.

Consumerist Leisure

One of the biggest consumer growth areas in the twentieth century was leisure. People were increasingly inclined to spend their money on being entertained. Sports, such as baseball in the United States, became major leisure activities, spawning a new industry of sports equipment manufacturing. Amusement parks arrived in the 1890s with the invention of the Ferris wheel and the roller coaster. The first movies were shown around 1900, and by 1920, families were seeing a movie every week. In consumerist leisure, as in all forms of consumerism, the latest thing was always the most popular, and trends in entertainment changed regularly.

Motivation to Consume

Is consumerism an inevitable consequence of human nature, or is it the result of historical developments in society? The

Shoppers enjoy the Myeong-Dong district nightlife in Seoul, South Korea.

Signs for fast-food restaurants, gas stations, and other outlets near Memphis, Tennessee, in the mid-1980s.

answer is probably a bit of both. Social changes from the 16th century onward laid the foundations for consumerism. However, the growth of consumerism today suggests that it appeals to something in our nature, such as our desire for comfort and status.

From the 16th century on, the European economy expanded rapidly, bringing vast profits to merchants and manufacturers. This new spending power, coupled with a desire to imitate social superiors, encouraged consumerism. The church, with its emphasis on simple living, had declined in power by the eighteenth century. A new movement emerged, known as the Enlightenment, which stressed improving our lives on Earth through the use of reason and science rather than preparing our souls for heaven. Thus, spending money on luxury goods became acceptable behavior.

In the nineteenth century, the Romantic movement of writers and artists praised physical beauty. People were inspired to buy clothes and products that enhanced their own beauty and that of their homes. In the twentieth century, one of the driving forces behind consumerism was the breakdown of class divisions, leading to a greater emphasis on status symbols, such as expensive houses, clothes, and cars.

Today, increased stress or boredom in personal and professional lives leads many to seek relief in shopping. This is often the case with lower-middle-class workers, such as secretaries and retail personnel, whose jobs involve a great deal of routine and stress. For example, in Germany between 1900 and 1930, the lower middle classes were most prolific in moviegoing, the purchase of radios, and cigarette smoking.

How Businesses Create Demand

One of the main ways producers create demand for products and services is by the following line of reasoning: "I can imagine it, therefore I want it. I want it, therefore I should have it. Because I should have it, I need it. Because I need it, I deserve it. Because I deserve it, I will do anything necessary to get it." This is the artificial internal drive that advertisers tap into. You can "imagine it" because ads will bombard your consciousness with its image until you move to step two, "I want it." And so on.

Demonstrators march through Toronto during an anti-globalization protest in 2016.

Advertisements are used by businesses to promote their products. The growth in the number of ads we see around us is a reflection of the power of consumerism in today's world.

Early ads tended to be wordy descriptions of products in newspapers. Then, in the late nineteenth century, as color printing became cheaper, the nature of advertising changed. Instead of using words to describe a product, advertisers aimed to make a visual impact: colorful posters appeared, containing attractive images and few words designed to appeal to people's emotions rather than to their reason.

The first advertising agencies were founded in New York City in 1870, and from that point on, promoting and selling goods became a more sophisticated and professional process. Today, companies spend a great deal of time researching their customers' desires and aspirations. They then use this information to create targeted advertisements. For example, a car manufacturer aiming to sell a car to 20-somethings might emphasize the speed and power of their vehicle, whereas the same company trying to sell a different model to an older age group might prefer to stress the car's safety features and roomy interior.

Growing Advertising Prevalence

The evidence of consumerism is all around us in the sheer number of ads that we see in our daily lives. Ads are everywhere: in addition to the usual places, they now appear on gas pumps, bathroom stalls, elevator walls, park benches, telephone booths, bus and train tickets, and even on space rockets. It has been estimated that we see up to 3,000 ads on an average day.

Sports events, stadiums, museums, parks, schools, theaters, and universities are now often named after their sponsors. People have now become walking advertisements, with designer labels visible on their clothing, including jeans and shirts. Celebrities are increasingly used to endorse products by using or wearing them at public appearances and even promoting them in interviews. Consumerism, in the form of ads, has become a highly visible part of our daily landscape.

 # Text-Dependent Questions

1. What were three ways consumerism changed since the 1920s?
2. Describe the progression of advertising as consumerism expanded.

 # Research Project

Using the Internet or your school library, research the topic of a 24-hour society, and answer the following question: "Is a 24-hour society beneficial or harmful to people?" Some claim that it is helpful to have the flexibility to shop, eat at a restaurant, have transportation, and do leisure activities at any time of the day or night because people have different schedules that might not match usual business hours. Others contend that a 24-hour society means countless people have to work long hours at unreasonable times. It also leads to a never-ending cycle of increasing consuming and producing that is harmful to people and society. Write a two-page report, using data you have found in your research to support your conclusion, and present it to your class.

2

How Consumerism Affects Society

C onsumerism has changed society in many different ways. The range and accessibility of products now on offer have served to make life more convenient and stimulating. However, the temptations of consumerism have also caused problems for many: families have been led into debt, health problems are on the increase, and crimes such as shoplifting are more prevalent.

Businesses have found innovative ways to make shopping a quicker, more convenient, and more pleasurable experience. Today, the department store has increasingly given way to the mall, a vast sprawl of stores in an enclosed area. With stores, restaurants, and entertainment venues now located in the same place, shopping has become even more associated with leisure. For those with little time on their hands, the Internet

A woman of the Masai tribe of Tanzania, Africa, uses a mobile phone. Consumerism has now invaded almost every aspect of human society, including traditional cultures.

and interactive TV allow shopping to be done at the click of a button.

Negative Aspects of Consumerism

Some of the social effects of consumerism have proven to be harmful. With so many more must-have products around for the fashion- or status-conscious, consumer spending is rising in greater proportion than people's income, leading many families into debt. In 2014, 69 percent of people US were in debt because of the amount they spent on products and services, not including mortgage payments for a home, while 62 percent were living from paycheck to paycheck. This problem has been made worse by the way some banks and loan companies encourage people to borrow money on their credit cards: 68 percent of those in debt said loans and credit cards enabled them to expand their purchases.

Consumerism can also be blamed for other social ills. The heavy advertising of delicious but unhealthy foods, such as sweets, soft drinks, potato chips, and fast food, has caused a significant rise in diet-related health problems, of which obesity (having excess amount of body fat) is the forerunner. In the

 Words to Understand in This Chapter

marketing—the process or technique of promoting, selling, and distributing a product or service.

obese—having excessive body fat.

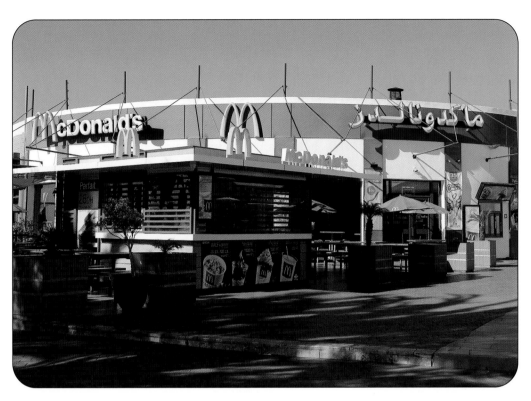

The spread of fast-food restaurants has been blamed for the worldwide rise in obesity. This McDonald's restaurant is located in the North African country of Morocco.

1990s, for the first time in human history, the world's population of overweight people was roughly the same as the number of underfed people—about 1.1 billion. In the United States in 2010, the National Institutes of Health reported more than one in three were *obese*, with the same rate for children. Obesity-related diseases, such as cardiovascular disease, cancer, diabetes, and high blood pressure, lead to 300,000 deaths per year in the United States.

The intense desires and frustrations that consumer culture can provoke in people are partly to blame for a steep increase in shoplifting. In the United States, there are approximately 27 million shoplifters (1 out of every 11 Americans) stealing around $36 million worth of goods per day, and more than 10 million have been caught in the last five years. 25 percent of shoplifters are kids, and 75 percent are adults; 55 percent of the adults reported beginning shoplifting in their teens. Personal and social pressures may be the main cause of this behavior, but it is a sign of our consumerist times that people choose to relieve these pressures by stealing goods from shops.

Credit cards enable people to "live beyond their means," by purchasing things that they don't truly need. Consequently, debt has become a problem for many families.

Museums, art galleries, and other tourist sites have adopted a consumerist attitude, with increasing space given over to shops selling souvenirs. In 2015, Americans spent an estimated $3 billion on souvenirs.

Consumerism and Romance

Consumerist attitudes are so entrenched in society that they even affect how people conduct their relationships. Take romance, for example: The concept of "dating" began around 1910, and the key difference between this and earlier forms of courtship was the involvement of some consumer activity, such as going to a movie or a restaurant. Young men and women came to judge their dates in consumerist terms. For instance, how generous was one partner to another? If a marriage pro-

Many couples now spend a lot of money on Valentine's Day by giving each other presents or by going out for "romantic" meals.

posal followed a date, an expensive ring would often be expected. As for weddings, there are now a range of services available for the special day, including flowers, catering, photographs, and videos.

Celebrations and Special Events

The effects of consumerism are not just limited to the way that we shop. Consumerism has spread to a number of other activities, such as vacations and celebrations. People have been buying Christmas presents since the 1830s, and by the end of the nineteenth century, Christmas shopping had become a huge commercial event. In the holiday season of 2013, US retailers generated $3.19 trillion in sales, which accounted for 19.2 percent of all retail sales that year. The average US consumer spent $830 on Christmas gifts in 2015.

The idea of celebrating birthdays with gift giving was another 19th-century invention. The first commercial Valentine cards were sold in the UK in 1855, and Mother's Day cards followed in 1914. Festivals and celebrations have increasingly become a vehicle to sell more products, and this has threatened to obscure the original meanings of these events.

Consumerism Effects beyond Shopping

Consumerist attitudes have also spread to politics. Today, political parties approach *marketing* companies to coordinate their election campaigns. Political candidates are sold like consumer products, adjusting their voice and appearance, their slogans, and sometimes even their policies, to create a brand that maximizes their appeal to the electorate.

Many universities are becoming more commercial in their attitudes as well, especially in the United States. Students and parents are often treated like customers, while courses and professors are rated for their quality. The demand for positive results from a college education has led to a rise in grade levels without any corresponding increase in the quality of work.

Consumerism has also affected sports in significant ways. Sports figures now compete not simply to win but also to get rich. The most successful can earn hundreds of millions from prize money and sponsorships. Businesses, eager to associate themselves with sports heroes, are happy to pay them generously to promote their products, which in turn produce greater profits. The temptations of sponsorship have been blamed for leading some athletes to take performance-enhancing drugs that enable them to play longer at higher levels.

Gender Differences

Until the end of the seventeenth century, most consumers were men, and products were directed almost exclusively at them. However, the eighteenth century witnessed a new interest in household items such as implements for cooking, dining, and cleaning—areas traditionally under women's control. This raised the status of women as consumers.

From the early nineteenth century on, men became less inclined to spend money on their appearance, and women began to lead the way in consumption of clothing and beauty products. In the 1890s, women's magazines started to appear, such as *Ladies' Home Journal*, *Woman's Home Companion*, and *Good Housekeeping*, with pictures of the latest fashions along with recipes and housekeeping tips.

By the 1910s, many young women had entered the labor market and for the first time enjoyed direct access to their own

 # Madam CJ Walker

In the early twentieth century, African-American women found it hard to participate in consumerism to the degree enjoyed by their white compatriots. They were not welcomed in many stores because of racial discrimination, and there were few beauty products designed specifically for them. The situation started to change with the arrival of Madam CJ Walker, who invented a hair-care formula for black women in the early 1900s. Unable to sell her product in stores, she began selling it door-to-door. She soon established a highly successful system of training and marketing (promoting, selling, and distributing) across the Southern and Midwestern United States. The sales agents and hairdressers she trained went on to train others, eventually widening distribution throughout the nation. Having started out—so she said— with half a dollar in her pocket, Walker's company achieved annual sales of $500,000 in 1919, the year she died.

money—an advantage they were unlikely to give up once they were married. Women started to become the dominant consumer group for food, clothing, and other everyday household goods.

Expansion of Marketing to Genders

In the 1920s, women began venturing into previously male-dominated areas such as cigarette smoking, alcohol, and cars. Marketers were quick to see this trend and began to produce products and advertisements that promoted qualities that were seen to be of interest to women. Car ads from this period, for example, began to focus on the product's color, ease of use, design, and upholstery.

Since the 1980s, men have begun to show interest in appearance-enhancing products at the same level as women. This has been revealed in the increasing number of men's fashion magazines, hair dyes, and cosmetics on the market. Men are also now rivaling women in their interest in cosmetic surgery. Sports retailers currently give far more floor and shelf space to fashion-related products than sports equipment.

Marketing toward Children

In the eighteenth century, products aimed directly at children began appearing, such as toys, games, and books. However, it was not until the twentieth century that children became major consumers in their own right, with the ability to buy items for themselves or persuade their parents to buy things for them. Today, children are often conditioned from an early age in the principles of consumerism. A major cause of sibling

Spokescharacters

During the 1980s, children's toy ads increasingly used well-known cartoon characters to sell products because there was evidence that this would boost sales. The owners of the characters' likenesses were happy to license them for this kind of use, and by 1987, 70 percent of toy ads used a "spokescharacter." The key to the success of this strategy is ensuring that the character is instantly recognizable to children. This is done by introducing the character to very young children through decorations, toys, and television. Today, this has led to all kinds of cross-promotion of products, with cartoon characters promoting products on TV, in magazines, and in fast-food restaurants.

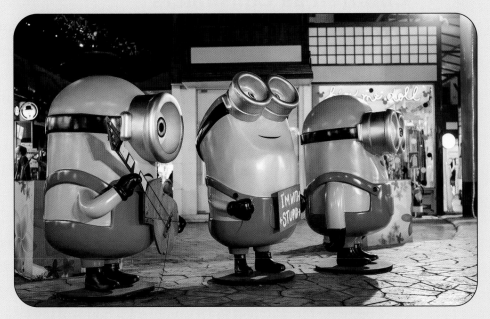

Oversized replicas of the "Minion" characters from a series of popular cartoon films are used to attract young shoppers to a store in Thailand.

rivalry in many homes stems from resentment that a brother or sister may have a new toy. If children are upset, their parents may try to bring peace by buying them a treat or an equivalent toy.

There is now a huge range of children's products—from potato chips and candy to athletic shoes and video games. Manufacturers and retailers are adept at packaging these items in bright colors to catch the eyes of children. They also place these goods on the lower shelves of their stores, at children's eye level and within easy reach, because research has shown that if a child touches a product, there is a greater chance that their parents will end up buying it.

Children as Consumers

Children are in many ways the ideal consumers, being more susceptible than adults to changes in style and fashion and providing a ready market for the latest crazes. Their influence on parental spending patterns continues to increase: Seventy-one percent of parents report asking for their children's opinions when purchasing a product; 85 percent of children choose what to eat at a fast-food restaurant; and in 2012, children's total buying power and influence reached $1.2 trillion. As a result, an enormous amount of money—$17 billion every year in the United States alone—is spent on advertising to children.

Television advertising is seen as a major reason for the rise in children's consumerism. in the United States, the average child between the ages of 8 to 18 watches 4.5 hours of television per day, compared to 6.5 hours in class on an average school day. They watch 40,000 commercials each year on average.

In 1991, the Scandinavian country of Sweden banned advertisements from primetime children's television programs, after research showed that children under the age of 10 were unable to tell the difference between a commercial and a program. The European Union is also considering regulating advertising aimed at children.

 # Text-Dependent Questions

1. Provide three examples of the negative impact of consumerism and explain each.
2. In the 1900s, non-traditional products were starting to be marketed toward different genders. Which products were directed at women? Which were directed at men?

 # Research Project

Using the Internet or your school library, research the topic of advertising toward children, and answer the following question: "Should restrictions be placed on advertising toward children?" Some believe there should be no restrictions because children have a right to learn what is available to them, and they should be able to make their own decisions. They know their preferences and need to learn how to make good choices for themselves. Advertisers should also have freedom to promote products in a free marketplace. Others argue that children are not able to distinguish between their needs and wants, and advertisers should not exploit this. They should not be exposed to sexual or violent media or ads for products such as alcohol or tobacco when watching children's programs. Ads directed at children also place extra pressure on parents to spend more money and further consumerism in themselves and their children. Write a two-page report, using data you have found in your research to support your conclusion, and present it to your class.

3

The Impact of Consumerism Internationally

So far we have looked at the effects of consumerism on wealthier Western nations. However, this phenomenon has spread to countries around the world, with an especially deep economic and social impact on poorer, developing nations.

Consumerism in Poorer Countries

Consumerism encourages people in developed countries to expect ever more choice and availability in the range of products in their stores, including products made in many different parts of the world. Products that were once considered luxuries—such as coffee, tea, chocolate, and tobacco—are now commonplace items in every supermarket. These products grow in tropical and subtropical regions, and they are low-priced

Thousands of tons of garbage are buried each day in landfill sites around the world. Bulldozers compact the waste, which is then covered with soil.

because of mass-production techniques and the relatively cheap cost of land and labor in these areas.

Large tracts of land in these countries have been bought up by Western corporations and turned over exclusively to growing "*cash crops*," as they are called, much of them for export to the West. Poorer nations often become overly dependent on one crop, and a dip in world demand can have devastating consequences for their economies. As major employers in these countries, multinational companies can dictate wages and land use. In many cases, the best agricultural land—which could be used to grow food for the local people—is turned over to non-food products, such as tobacco and flowers, for export.

The mechanized nature of mass farming has left less work available for rural workers. Hunger and poverty has driven many to the cities in search of jobs, creating slums and shanty towns on city outskirts, with consequent health problems. About one-third of the world's urban population lives in slums,

 Words to Understand in This Chapter

cash crop—a crop (such as tobacco or cotton) in high demand that is grown to be sold rather than for use by the farmer.

decadent—used to describe someone with low morals and a great love of pleasure, money, and/or fame.

equitable—just or fair, dealing fairly and equally with everyone.

fair trade—a movement whose goal is to help producers in developing countries to get a fair price for their products so as to reduce poverty, provide for the ethical treatment of workers and farmers, and promote environmentally sustainable practices.

A shanty town in Brazil. Such places have little access to clean water and sanitation, and people living here are prone to diseases such as cholera and typhoid.

but in regions like sub-Saharan Africa, that figure jumps to 61.7 percent.

Influence of Multinational Companies on Governments

Today, most multinational companies contract out the production of their goods to businesses in developing countries where labor is cheap. For example, in 2010, the clothing manufacturer Gap Inc. bought its goods from 1,200 factories based in 44 countries around the world.

Because they do not actually own these businesses, multinational companies can easily switch production to other countries if economic conditions are more favorable elsewhere. This gives them a great deal of power over governments, which are eager to keep jobs in their countries. They sometimes use this power to influence government policy. For example, the Gambian government was forced to abolish certain restrictions on developing the tourist industry following pressure from multinational companies.

The Beef Trade

The rise of fast-food restaurants since the 1950s has turned beef into a major consumer product. The biggest global fast-food chain, McDonald's, now has about 36,000 restaurants in over 100 countries worldwide and is the US's largest purchaser of beef. To satisfy worldwide demand for this product, millions of acres in Latin America have been given over to pasture for cattle or to grow grain for cattle feed. In Brazil, this has left some 4.8 million rural families landless.

Hidden Costs of Coffee

Coffee is the world's second-most valuable traded consumer product in the world, behind only petroleum. Twenty-five million farmers and coffee workers in over 50 countries are involved in producing coffee. Upscale coffee chains such as Costa, Starbucks, and Caffe Nero, are commonplace on city streets, selling a wide variety of coffees with names that have now entered the general vocabulary, such as "caramel macchiato" and "white chocolate mocha." Starbucks alone had 21,366

Fair Trade Coffee

A drian Lovett, Campaigns Director at the social justice organization Oxfam, said "The [coffee] companies know there is terrible suffering at the heart of their business, and yet they do virtually nothing to help. It's time to shame them and change them."

One key movement that has helped combat exploitation in the coffee industry is *fair trade*. Prior to fair trade, prices were determined by the International Coffee Organization, based on the International Coffee Agreement of 1962 negotiated at the United Nations. It set limits on the amount of coffee traded between countries so there would be no excess supply or drop in price.

Alternative trade organizations (ATOs) emerged in Europe and the US to promote grassroots development through direct, *equitable* trade, now known as fair trade. These organizations bought directly from producers in developing countries and paid the producers a fair price while providing trading experience and teaching them how to write a profitable contract. The first ATO to bring fair trade to the coffee industry was called Max Havelaar in the Netherlands. It helped artificially raise coffee prices, even if there was a coffee surplus, in order to ensure high enough wages for a workers and farmers to turn a profit.

Coffee chains such as Starbucks are making huge profits as the price of their main raw material slumps.

outlets worldwide in 2014.

The instant variety of coffee is also wildly popular. Every second of the day, an estimated 5,500 cups of Nescafe, the world's leading instant coffee brand, are drunk in 180 countries around the globe. Yet the coffee business is also an example of the dark side of consumerism, where greed for profits has left farmers in the producer nations in dire poverty.

The world's four largest coffee companies, "the Big Four," are Kraft, Sara Lee, Proctor & Gamble, and Nestle. Each owns coffee brands worth over a billion dollars, yet coffee farmers receive just five percent of the price consumers pay. Since 1992, coffee production has increased twice as fast as coffee consumption, leading to millions of bags of unused coffee in warehouses around the world. All this excess has driven prices down. The big four coffee companies have tried to limit the impact of coffee's low price on their profits by buying coffee as cheaply as possible. In 1997, when the currency of Vietnam lost its value, multinational companies took advantage of the cheap prices and began buying their coffee from Vietnam. This forced traditional growers in Africa and Central America to reduce their prices too. As a result, the price of coffee dropped

Workers on a coffee plantation in southeastern Brazil, where many farmers depend on the income from this product.

by 50 percent between 2000 and 2003, hitting a 30-year low.

It left millions of coffee farmers around the world in situations close to starvation. Countries like Uganda, Ethiopia, and Rwanda, which depended on coffee for half of their export revenue, faced economic collapse. The number of Ethiopians in need of emergency food aid rose from 6 million to about 15 million, partly as a result of the crisis. Some farmers in South and Central America were so desperate they switched from growing coffee to growing coca, the raw material for cocaine. Others migrated to the cities in search of work.

Currently, coffee chains like Starbucks and Costa tend to pay fairer prices to coffee growers, but their contribution has not been sufficient to lift farmers out of poverty.

Consumerism in Non-Western Countries

Consumerism began in the West, and Western countries remain the biggest consumers by far. Nevertheless, over the past 50 years, consumerism has had a strong influence on countries outside Western Europe and the United States, where it is associated with Western—particularly American—culture.

For most of the twentieth century, Russia formed the major territory of the Soviet Union, a communist country in which the state controlled all industry, and Western-style consumerism was almost unheard of. When the Soviet Union collapsed in 1991, the new government introduced a free-market capitalist system, similar to the one that operates in the West. Russian businesspeople, known as "new Russians," grew very

Although the production of tobacco products is labor intensive, companies are able to keep their costs down by using cheap labor from poorer countries. These workers are preparing cigars in the Partagas factory in Havana, Cuba.

A busy store in Moscow. Since the collapse of communism in the Soviet Union in 1991, some Russians have become extremely rich and able to buy a wide range of luxury goods.

rich and began to use their newly earned wealth to indulge in consumerist purchases.

The Russian economy struggled during the 1990s, however, and large parts of Russian society remained poor. Some felt resentful of the showy displays of the new Russians, and others were even nostalgic for the days of the Soviet Union. Today, consumerism remains confined to a fairly narrow band of Russian society, although it has begun to increase.

Western Influence in Japan

Many East Asian countries have been eager to embrace the consumerism of the West, especially Japan—the most Americanized of non-Western countries.

When Tokyo Disneyland opened in 1984, the Japanese owners copied the original theme park in Los Angeles as closely as possible—including park areas such as Frontierland (which was renamed Westernland) and characters such as Mickey Mouse, who has become very familiar to most Japanese children. By 1988, the theme park was attracting 13 million tourists every year, making it one of the most popular attractions in the whole country. In 2014, 17 million visitors attended Tokyo Disneyland.

Gift giving is important in Japanese culture, so the gift shops located on Tokyo Disneyland's Main Street are particularly busy. For similar reasons, the festivities of Christmas (in its modern, commercial form) is extremely popular in Japan, even though it is not a Christian country.

The Japanese are also frequently among the first to take up new technologies. For example, picture phones were launched there in 2001, before they were introduced in Europe and the US, and by 2003, they had become an established part of Japanese youth culture.

Consumerism in China

Despite having a communist government, China has been moving toward a free-market economy since 1978, leading to a growing middle class with a large appetite for goods and services. China's economy, boosted by this increase in middle class wealth, is undergoing a sizable shift in consumption driven by a new generation of young, prosperous consumers who are rising in social class, less price-sensitive, and able to display their success through their purchases. Among the aspirations of middle class in China are a high quality of life, the best education, and a secure retirement, which has led retailers to expand the industries of tourism, luxury brands, and technology.

Another factor that may have contributed to consumerism in Chinese families is the government's strict one-child-per-family policy, an effort to control the rapidly growing population in a country that already has 1.36 billion people. This may have led some parents to invest even more heavily in their only child through consumer goods.

Reaction of the Islamic Middle East to Consumerism

In the West, the rise of consumerism corresponded to a decline in the prevalence of Christianity. In the Middle East, however, the religion of Islam remains a powerful influence in the day-to-day lives of millions of people, and this has acted as a severe brake on the development of a consumer culture. The governments and large portions of the population in these countries regard the Western lifestyle as *decadent* and corrupt. Drinking alcohol and gambling, for example, are against Islamic law, and many Muslims believe that women should dress conservatively, covering their heads and majority of their bodies in public. They are also shocked by the sexual and violent nature of many of today's Hollywood movies.

Despite these attitudes, consumerism has penetrated some

Shoppers walk through a mall in Istanbul, Turkey.

Islamic societies. Turkey and Egypt both have a sizeable urban middle class that enjoys spending money on consumer goods, both locally produced and imported. In 2015, for example, Turks bought about 900,000 new cars. Even in very strict Islamic countries, such as Saudi Arabia, consumerism has had some impact. Oil revenues have made certain sections of Saudi society very rich, and some people enjoy spending their money on luxury cars and shopping sprees in Western cities.

A busy shopping center in Dubai, United Arab Emirates.

African Consumerism

The reaction of African countries to consumerism has been mixed. Some have been eager to adopt Western lifestyles, while other more conservative countries see consumerism as a threat to their traditional culture. Though there have been only a few serious efforts to limit Western influence, some countries' leaders have tried, such as the Zambian government discussing ideas about banning imports of Western clothing in the 1990s. African TV stations carry ads for Western products, but little care has been taken to adapt the messages for local audiences, many of whom are unused to Western "marketing-speak" and tend to regard the ads with skepticism or confusion. One villager, for example, reported his bewilderment at the slogan, "Coke adds life," when he felt no extra "life" after drinking a bottle.

 # Text-Dependent Questions

1. Describe negative consequences for poorer nations dependent on cash crops for their economy.
2. What caused the coffee crisis in the early 2000s, and in what ways did it impact poorer countries involved?
3. What are two factors that led to a rise in consumerism in China?

 # Research Project

Using the Internet or your school library, research the topic of fair trade and working conditions in source countries, and answer the following question: "Are consumers who buy products responsible if producers exploit their workers?" Some think that with their dollars, consumers have the ultimate vote on what products are on the market and how producers make them. If they were willing to pay a little more for fair trade goods or refused to buy products made by underpaid workers in poor conditions, producers would be influenced to raise standards for their employees. Consumers do have power, and thus, responsibility, regarding the exploitation of workers. Others say that because the producers are the employers, they have the full responsibility on whether or not their workers are exploited. Consumers simply buy goods or services for themselves and are far removed from the production process. They may not know the working conditions for those who make the product and cannot be blamed in the matter. Write a two-page report, using data you have found in your research to support your conclusion, and present it to your class.

4

Consumerism and the Environment

Consumerism has taken a growing toll on the environment. One main issue is the waste produced by large-scale manufacturing and consumption. This has contributed to the contamination of rivers, poisoning of soils, and pollution of air in many towns and cities.

Growing Waste from Consumer Products

Massive quantities of garbage are thrown away each year—an inevitable byproduct of the consumer culture. Much of this is non-*biodegradable*. The developed world is responsible for most of this waste.

In the Los Angeles area alone, 10 metric tons of plastic fragments—such as grocery bags, straws and soda bottles—are

Every day one in four Americans visits a fast-food restaurant. The mass production of beef to feed this demand has taken a toll on the rainforests.

dumped into the Pacific Ocean every day. The average American throws away approximately 185 pounds of plastic per year, with 50 percent of the plastic used just once before being tossed. Over the last 10 years, more plastic has been produced than in the entire last century, and enough is discarded each year to circle the earth four times.

The direct impact on living creatures is serious: 1 million sea birds and 100,000 marine mammals are killed every year from plastic in the oceans, and 93 percent of Americans age six or older test positive for the plastic chemical BPA.

The United States, with less than 5 percent of the world's population, uses about one-quarter of the world's fossil fuel resources. The Earth has 1.9 hectares of biologically productive land per person to supply resources and absorb wastes—yet the average person today already uses 2.3 hectares. These "ecological footprints" range from 9.7 hectares claimed by the average American to 0.47 hectares used by the average Mozambican.

Each time a car is driven, it emits carbon dioxide, hydrocar-

 Words to Understand in This Chapter

biodegradable—capable of being broken down especially into harmless products by the action of living things (as microorganisms).

livestock—farm animals such as cows, horses, and pigs that are kept, raised, and used by people.

slash and burn—agriculture characterized by cutting down and burning trees and plants in order to clear an area of land and grow crops on it for usually a brief time.

The increased number of cars on the roads in developing countries like China, India, Brazil, and Russia create high levels of air pollution. At times, the air in Beijing and other Chinese cities is extremely unhealthy to breathe, and people who can afford it stay inside where they have expensive air filtration systems.

bons, and other pollutants into the air, which can cause asthma, bronchitis, pneumonia, and heart disease. The UN reports there are 3.3 million premature deaths per year from air pollution, three-quarters of which are from pollution-related strokes and heart attacks. Despite a concerted effort toward more fuel-efficient transportation, the US vehicle market still causes twice as much air pollution as Europe and Japan.

Pollution from Current Consumer Trends

One reason for the increasing amount of waste is the trend toward "disposable" items—products designed to be used once before being thrown away. Fragile or edible products usually come with large amounts of packaging, which further adds to garbage. The problem is not helped by the planned obsolescence of products such as computers and cell phones. Every year, fully functioning products like these get thrown out in favor of the latest models.

Mass consumerism obviously depends on the mass production of goods, and the manufacturing process itself is often a major cause of waste. Much of the waste produced in the manufacturing process is dumped directly into rivers and oceans or released as gases into the air. Some of this industrial waste is hazardous to human, animal, and plant life. About 80,000 different chemicals are regularly used in modern factories, of

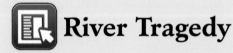 **River Tragedy**

In January 2000, 3.5 million cubic feet of highly toxic cyanide leaked from a Romanian gold mine into the local river network. Almost all fish and animal life was wiped out on the Tisza River which flows through Romania and Hungary. Fish were killed as far away as the Danube, several hundred miles from the site of the leakage. It will be many years before life on these rivers fully recovers.

Millions of disposable plastic bottles wind up polluting the oceans each year, causing damage to marine ecosystems.

Internet shopping sites have become a major force for the spread of consumerism—and globalization—in the world today.

which less than 20 percent have been tested for harmful effects; many of these chemicals are dangerous in themselves, while others produce hazardous wastes during their use. Major rivers, like the Rhine in Western Europe and the Ganges in India, are so polluted from industrial waste that wildlife has disappeared along large stretches of their length.

Agricultural Impact on the Rainforests

Rainforests are a valuable resource for food (vegetables, nuts, coffee), medicine (chemicals from plants are used to treat hundreds of illnesses), and clean air. rainforests absorb carbon dioxide in the air and produce oxygen that humans and animals breathe, but deforestation removes masses of valuable trees, contributing to a 12 to 15 percent increase of all greenhouse gas emissions each year.

Consumer-driven demand for more food at cheaper prices has encouraged large areas of tropical rainforest to be turned over to intensive agriculture. rainforest soil is less rich than soils in other areas because most of the nutrients are stored in the trees and plants themselves. When the trees are cut down or burned to clear the area for farmland, most of the nutrients

This hillside in Ecuador has been cleared using slash-and-burn techniques, and planted with corn.

Clearing of the rainforests in places like Brazil, Indonesia, and West Africa is believed to contribute to harmful climate change.

disappear with them. The fragile soil is rapidly exhausted through cultivation, forcing farmers to cut down or burn even more forest and start all over again. This wasteful method of agriculture is known as *"slash and burn."*

Grazing cattle also do a great deal of damage to rainforest areas. In India, nomadic cattle farmers have been forced away from their traditional pastures by the establishment of permanent farms. Their cattle now graze on rainforest margins, destroying much of the plant life there. Of India's 300 million cattle, 90 million live on rainforest land. Cattle have also caused problems for the South American rainforests: in the 1970s and 1980s, Brazilian landowners were given tax incentives to clear massive areas of rainforest in order to raise cattle for the enormous beef market in the United States. However, this policy led to the destruction of so great an area of rainforest that it has now been stopped.

Industrial Impact on Rainforests

Water is plentiful in tropical regions, and governments in these regions often use this resource to generate electricity by building huge hydroelectric dams. Some of these dams are used to power large-scale industrial processes such as steel production and aluminum smelting. However, building dams often requires the flooding of large areas of rainforest.

Rainforest land is frequently mined for precious minerals, including silver and gold. Mining operations cause immense damage to the local environment: large areas must be cleared and access roads built; heavy machinery flattens the soil; and local rivers are often polluted by the poisonous substances used

Livestock farming has become an industrialized business in many parts of the world.

in the mining process. In the gold mines of the Amazon in South America, mercury is used to separate gold from gravel. To extract 100 tons of gold, at least 130 tons of mercury—which can cause damage to the nervous, digestive, and immune systems—is released into the environment.

Livestock Farming

Intensive *livestock* breeding for the fast-food industry has had a major environmental impact. Thirty percent of the world's ice-free land is occupied by chickens, pigs, and cattle eventually used for food. Livestock are responsible for about 18 percent of human-caused greenhouse gases in the form of methane from manure.

Compared to crop farming, livestock farming is also inefficient in terms of water usage: water is necessary to not only cultivate the 1.3 billion tons of grain used for feeding livestock but also for the animals to drink directly.

 # Text-Dependent Questions

1. Explain how two current trends in consumerism are harming the environment?
2. Why are rainforests beneficial to humans, and what factors are leading to their destruction?

 # Research Project

Using the Internet or your school library, research the topic of ecological footprints, and answer the following question: "Can individuals or the government make a bigger difference in reducing our ecological footprint in the world?" Some contend that individuals have more power in helping reduce our ecological footprint because they can make environmentally-friendly choices in the transportation they take, their energy usage, and the products they buy. People can quickly change their consumption patterns, unlike the government, which takes a long time to make changes. A collection of individuals making good choices for the environment is our best hope. Others argue that the government can make a bigger impact by regulating large companies that produce harmful chemicals or making laws that restrict emissions from cars. The government can also enact programs that lead people to recycle more or plant trees to improve the environment. The government can cause change in masses of people and large companies. Write a two-page report, using data you have found in your research to support your conclusion, and present it to your class.

5

The Debate about Consumerism

As we have seen, consumerism has had a major impact on society, human rights, and the environment. Most people are happy to go on enjoying its benefits. Some, however, see consumerism as something harmful and dangerous that must be opposed. This has led to the formation of anti-consumerist groups.

In the 1960s, the hippie movement was made up mostly of young people who rejected the consumerist lifestyle of their parents. They formed alternative communes based on a more natural way of life in which personal relationships mattered more than possessions. The movement eventually faded and, ironically, certain products of that era, such as colorful clothing and rock music, have become consumer items themselves.

More effective and long-lasting than the hippie movement

Shopping malls are now found in almost every major town and city in the world. The world's largest mall, in Dongguan, China, has more than 1,000 stores.

was the environmentalist, or green, movement which began to gain momentum in the 1970s. Environmental groups, such as Greenpeace and Friends of the Earth, urged governments, businesses, and individuals to take better care of the natural world, and consumerism has been a major target of their criticism. Environmentalists have tried to encourage people to think more carefully about how they consume. They have brought attention to the plight of the world's rainforests, the effects of air pollution, and many other problems caused by consumerism. While the green movement has been successful in raising awareness of environmental problems, it has had only a limited impact on consumerism.

In the late 1990s, a new movement arose protesting *globalization*, the trend toward global economic interdependence due to the increasing flow of money around the world. Protesters claimed that globalization brought wealth and power to large, multinational companies at the expense of ordinary people.

 Words to Understand in This Chapter

chador—a large cloth worn as a combination head covering, veil, and shawl, usually by Muslim women especially in Iran.

globalization—the development of an increasingly integrated worldwide economy marked especially by free trade, free flow of capital, and the tapping of cheaper foreign labor markets.

Islamism—a conservative movement advocating for government and society to align with laws and social values prescribed in the early days of the Islamic religion (the seventh century CE).

sustainable—able to be used without being completely used up or destroyed.

Activists in New Zealand march to protest the Trans-Pacific Partnership, a free trade agreement signed in 2016.

Many blame this on the culture of consumerism in the West, which encourages multinational companies to continue with their exploitative policies. They argue that the only way to change the behavior of these producers is for consumers to stop buying products that are manufactured using methods that harm the environment or exploit people.

Opposition to Consumerism in Non-Western Countries

In non-Western countries, consumerism is often associated with Westernization—the global spread of Western—mainly

Smart Shopping

Bob Horowitz of Sustainable Enterprises has promoted the idea of intentionally purchasing for the benefit of the environment: "People say if we stop buying so many things, the economy will collapse. I say we are buying the wrong things. If we buy high-quality, *sustainably*-made goods—even if we buy fewer of them—the economy will be stronger and more stable than ever. Let's face the facts, an economy based on the increasing consumption of resources is only temporary, because the amount of resources on the planet, without a doubt, is finite. Once the Earth is all used up, we don't simply move to the next valley."

American—culture. This can be seen by the appearance of Western fashions, pop music, Hollywood movies, satellite television, and McDonald's restaurants in almost every country of the world. In Mexico, for example, the local film industry went from making 100 films a year to just 10 films in 1998, mainly because of competition from Hollywood. In the remote West Pokot region of Kenya, young people have virtually abandoned traditional dress in favor of pants and T-shirts.

Consumerism and Westernization have understandably caused resentment in parts of South America, Africa, and Asia, where people fear the loss of their own national or cultural identity. However, there have been few coordinated efforts to reject these processes. This is partly because Westernization has also brought economic benefits to non-Western countries.

Tourism, for example, is one kind of consumerism that has helped certain ethnic groups, such as the Masai of Kenya and the Padaung of Myanmar and Thailand, which have been strengthened by the interest of tourists.

Response to Consumerism in Islamic Countries

The most significant non-Western, anti-consumerist movement is *Islamism*, which is a powerful force in many Muslim countries across the Middle East, South Asia, and North Africa. Islamism, which is also known as Islamic fundamental-

Religious leaders in Iran have denounced Western consumerism as being against Islamic principles.

ism, is a movement to return society to a "pure" state by eliminating Western influences and corruption. Islamists regard consumerism as a product of Western decadence and put pressure on their governments to ban Western products and ads.

In Iran, consumerism has been denounced by the ruling Islamist Muslim clerics, and, while wealthier Iranians have been attracted to Western luxuries, many ordinary Iranians see the consumerist attitudes of the West as alien to their culture. Anti-consumerism was a major force behind the Iranian revolution in 1979, which brought an Islamist government to power in the country. One of the first acts of the new government was to insist that women give up their Western clothing and conceal themselves in the traditional *chador*—a dark garment that covers the head and body.

Consumerism has also been criticized by Islamist move-

 Fewer Things, Greater Enjoyment

The anti-consumerist website Overcoming Consumption posted, "Having fewer things means enjoying what you have more and actually getting to use it, thereby raising its intrinsic value. The less clutter that one has in one's surroundings, the fewer distractions there are from the essentials such as family, friends, food, nature, and study. With less clutter, one needs a smaller space in which to live comfortably, and thus, one needs to work less to pay rent to store things. If you haven't used something in the last year, how much likelihood is there that you ever will use it?"

ments in Turkey, Algeria, and Egypt. For example, in July 2001, conservative religious authorities issued a condemnation of the Egyptian version of the American game show *Who Wants to be a Millionaire?*

Negative Aspects of Consumerism

Consumerism is both a positive and a negative force in today's society. It has contributed to a great improvement in most people's quality of life and helped to break down social divisions while creating a sense of global belonging. However, consumerism also has undeniable environmental, social, and cultural costs.

Consumerism, as already discussed, has caused significant problems because of the way goods are produced and sold around the globe. It also encourages a shallow and materialistic approach to life: It emphasizes the importance of buying things over activities such as sports, artistic creativity, or study. Our energies can become focused on satisfying our material desires rather than on developing our minds or spirits.

Ads attempt to manipulate us by encouraging needs that never existed before and by making us more conformist in our choices. This mentality leads us to buy similar products, and in this sense, consumerism can be seen as the enemy of diversity and individualism. It has contributed to a more narrow range in people's lifestyles, desires, and aspirations.

Benefits of Consumerism

Consumerism is certainly not all bad. It has contributed to a general rise in people's standard of living. It has encouraged producers to create cheaper variations on products that had previously been available only to the very rich and introduced people on lower incomes to luxuries and comforts they could never have otherwise afforded. It has also given a higher profile to consumers as a group and promoted the right to high-quality service from suppliers.

Consumerism does not always mean the imposition of Western styles on other cultures. Despite the power of Western multinational companies, there are plenty of examples of homegrown consumerism in non-Western societies. Japan and India have managed to become consumerist without totally surrendering to Western values. India, for example, now has the world's largest film industry, Bollywood.

Some consumerist products have managed to travel successfully from non-Western to Western countries. For example, Japan has successfully begun to export its own cultural goods to Europe, the United States, the Middle East, and other parts of Asia with products like Pokemon, anime comics, soap operas, and computer games. African styles of music and fashion have become popular in the West, and foods, such as curry from India and sushi from Japan, have now become established favorites.

Making Consumerism Less Costly

Most of the groups who protest against consumerism accept that they can never defeat it entirely. Society has grown too accustomed to a certain standard of living to give it all up voluntarily. However, there are some things that can be done to curb the most damaging effects of consumerism. Individuals

Children playing a video game. Commercials showing children having fun using products such as video games can convey several messages, such as "this product is cool" and "you are inferior if you do not have this product."

can take more care over how they consume while governments and international agencies can publicize the risks of over-consumption and regulate the exploitative practices of multinational companies.

There are various ways in which people can adapt their lives without completely rejecting consumerism that would be less costly to other people and the planet. They can buy products that do not harm the environment or animals or exploit workers in their manufacturing: free-range eggs, for example, or cosmetics that have not been tested on animals. Organic meat is both healthier to the consumer and kinder to animals and the environment than processed meat bought in many fast-food restaurants. Ethical consumers can make sure that what they buy was produced by a member of a fair trade organization, which will ensure that a fair price is paid to farmers.

Consumerism has given society a taste for luxuries—things which are nice, but not strictly necessary. To limit the negative effects of overconsumption, consumers could ask themselves, "What do I need?" rather than "What do I want?" when they enter a store. In particular, they could limit their use of disposable products, which use up the planet's resources and add to the problem of waste. Clothing and electronics can be used until they are worn out and not thrown away just because a new fashion or model is available. Air pollution can be reduced by buying a bicycle, using public transportation, and driving only when necessary. Waste could be cut by turning off a running faucet, reusing containers and packaging, buying loose fruit and vegetables rather than packaged ones, and buying in bulk.

Governments could also do more to reduce the problems of

consumerism. For example, they could encourage industries to develop efficient technologies to deal with waste and pollution, educate children about the costs of consumerism, regulate advertising to children, and put pressure on companies to pay fairer wages to workers in developing countries.

 # Text-Dependent Questions

1. Name two anti-consumerist movements that started in the 1960s and 1970s, and describe characteristics of each.
2. Provide two drawbacks and two benefits to consumerism.
3. What are five practical ways people can reduce the negative impact of consumerism?

 # Research Project

Using the Internet or your school library, research the topic of simple living versus materialism, and answer the following question: "Is life better with fewer material possessions or more?" Some believe that fewer possessions means materials will be less of a priority, and more important things, like relationships and meaningful causes, will come to the forefront. It leads to less dependence on technology, financial burden, and harm to the environment. A simpler lifestyle is a better lifestyle. Others maintain that being able to buy goods and services improves the quality of life. Having a better home or technology makes things more convenient and saves time that can be devoted to friends and family. There will also be more to enjoy with others, making life more full and enjoyable. Write a two-page report, using data you have found in your research to support your conclusion, and present it to your class.

6

The Future of Consumerism

How will consumerism change and develop in the years to come? The culture of consumerism is so ingrained in modern society that it will be an uphill climb to see any dramatic adjustment of lifestyles toward more sustainable consumption.

The process of globalization looks set to continue, with increasingly similar products and brands available around the globe—albeit with regional variations. Advertising will become ever more sophisticated and far-reaching. But consumerism also faces a number of challenges, such as religious revivals in different parts of the world, anti-globalization protests, and increasing gaps between rich and poor.

Athletes like Tom Brady have come to symbolize the changing views of men and women in consumer advertising. Although respected by most men as a top football player, Brady is also portrayed as being interested in fashion and looking good. Consequently, he has been employed to sell fashion and beauty products.

Conflict from Consumerism

Many religious people have strong concerns about consumerism because it focuses attention on material gain rather than on spiritual development. With a revival of religious faith in many parts of the world, the conflict between religion and consumerism is likely to continue. This is especially the case with the rise of Islamism in the Muslim world. In the 1990s, the arrival of US military forces in Kuwait led to a growing interest in consumerism among the local people, but the military presence also inspired the hostility of Islamic conservatives.

Conservative Christians tend to not be strongly opposed to consumerism in general, and, in fact, many *fundamentalist* Christian preachers enjoy a wealthy, consumerist lifestyle themselves. They reserve their condemnation for those aspects of consumerism regarded as sinful, such as getting drunk on alcohol, gambling, drug dealing, and prostitution. Religious faith can coexist with consumerism, but not without tensions. For some, religion may provide an alternative to consumerism.

The anti-globalization movement is still in its early stages, and it is unclear how big it will grow. It is currently weakened

 Words to Understand in This Chapter

fundamentalist—a movement or attitude stressing strict and literal adherence to a set of basic principles.

anti-capitalist—a person who is opposed to a capitalist economic system, and wants to replace capitalism with a different system.

Protesters hold signs advocating for an increase in the minimum wage during a 2015 rally in Los Angeles.

by its lack of focus and leadership, but one issue that unites human rights activists, environmentalists, *anti-capitalists*, and others that make up the movement is concern over consumerism and its effects. All of these groups believe that protecting people's rights and the environment is more important than keeping consumers satisfied. It is unlikely that the anti-globalization movement will grow strong enough to put consumerism into reverse, but it may be able to place sufficient pressure on companies worried about their public image to make them change their ways.

An hungry child collects rubbish in a landfill in Mozambique. There is a growing gap between wealthy and poor people worldwide.

Will Consumerism Make the World More United?

Another shadow hanging over consumerism is the gap between rich and poor, which has steadily widened over the past 30 years. Oxfam reported that the richest 1 percent of the world's population owned 48 percent of the world's wealth in 2014. One in nine people do not have enough to eat, and 896 million people live on less than $1.90 per day. Consumerism has left behind vast portions of Africa and even many living in the developed West. in the United States, the bottom 10 percent of income earners devote 42 percent of their spending to housing and an additional 17 percent to food—about 60 percent of their total spending. By contrast, the wealthiest 10 percent spend only 31 percent of their income on housing and 11 percent to

 # Neuromarketing

In the future, consumers may find that companies are well informed about what they want to buy. A new tool is available which may allow companies to map the consumer's mind while they are shopping. Neuromarketing, as this process is called, was developed by a company in Atlanta. It involves scanning people's brains to record their thoughts and feelings as they look at pictures of products and ads. The goal is to bridge the gap between what consumers want and what they actually find on the shelves of their store. Technology such as this can only strengthen consumerism in times to come.

Correcting the Imbalance

Author Anup Shah wrote a wakeup call in *Behind Consumption and Consumerism:* "If the trends continue without change—not redistributing from high-income to low-income consumers, not shifting from polluting to cleaner goods and production technologies, not promoting goods that empower poor producers, not shifting priority from consumption for conspicuous display to meeting basic needs—today's problems of consumption and human development will worsen."

food—closer to 40 percent of total spending. Whether this huge inequality can be sustained is open to question. It may well lead to new forms of protest.

Factors that Spread Consumerism

Despite these question marks, the likelihood is that consumerism will continue to spread, as more people around the world seek to define themselves, at least in part, by the things they buy. India, Turkey, Mexico, and Brazil have sizeable middle classes that already enjoy a consumerist lifestyle. China and Russia are not far behind in their consumerist aspirations. Globalization will help move this process forward. Young people all over the world, from Manchester in the UK to Manila in the Philippines, are already wearing the same styles of dress, listening to the same musical artists, and supporting the same sports teams.

This sense of a global consumerist culture, especially in the world's urban environments, is likely to intensify over the coming years for a number of reasons: First, media communications is increasingly international in scope with a small number of giant corporations dominating the world's television networks, music, films, newspapers, and magazines. Second, the Internet gives unprecedented numbers of people access to the very latest in popular culture, accelerating the spread of new consumerist trends around the globe. Third, English—the language of 55.5 percent of Internet sites—will be learned and spoken by ever increasing numbers of people. Already two in

Spectators watch as costumed monks perform at a Buddhist monastery in the Asian country of Bhutan. In recent years the conservative Buddhist government of Bhutan has attempted to purge the country of foreign cultures and consumerism.

Consumerism affects all parts of the world, both human and natural, in many different ways.

ten people around the world speak English, and this trend toward shared language will only help the spread of a global consumerist culture.

For all its faults, consumerism is certainly here to stay. Regulating it is a challenge to be faced by everyone, from global organizations to individuals. Consumerism is clearly a part of human nature, but, ultimately, it should serve the needs of humans without placing itself in conflict with nature.

 # Text-Dependent Questions

1. How have different religious communities reacted to the rise of consumerism?
2. Name and explain three factors that will likely spread global consumerism in the coming years.

 # Research Project

Using the Internet or your school library, research the topic of global consumerism, and answer the following question: "Will consumerism continue to grow at a rapid pace in the world?" Some think that consumerism will continue to spread as technology allows more access to products and services worldwide, and large, untapped markets like Russia and China are increasingly reached by producers. Others say that the current pace of consumerism is unsustainable. It has already met concerted resistance from groups such as environmentalists, anti-capitalists, and Islamists, and it is likely to meet even greater opposition in the future. The overuse of resources and damage to the environment will force people and countries to make changes in their consumption patterns. Write a two-page report, using data you have found in your research to support your conclusion, and present it to your class.

Statistics of Inequality

Wealth Distribution

In 2014, the richest 1 percent held 48 percent of global wealth, and the next wealthiest 19 percent owned another 46.5 percent, leaving the remaining 80 percent of the world with just 5.5 percent of global wealth. The bottom 80 percent had an average wealth of $3,851 per adult—1/700th of the average wealth of the 1 percent.

Source: Oxfam International, 2015

Consumption Distribution

The world's richest 20 percent account for 76.6 percent of total private consumption. The world's poorest 20 percent consume only 1.5 percent.

Source: World Bank Development Indicators, 2008

Consumption per Capita, by Country

Country	Consumption in US dollars
United States	$30,872
United Kingdom	$25,340
Denmark	$23,197
Japan	$22,408
Canada	$22,166
Australia	$21,782
Germany	$21,654
Hong Kong	$21,403
France	$19,927
Italy	$17,297
Israel	$13,234
Poland	$6,579
Turkey	$5,969
Mexico	$5,827
Argentina	$5,648
Russia	$4,539
South Africa	$3,981
Brazil	$3,909
China	$1,307
Egypt	$1,119
Indonesia	$1,073
Algeria	$1,014
India	$691
Nigeria	$620

Source: The World Bank,
Household final consumption expenditure per capita, 2013

World Consumption of Consumer Products

Product	Percentage of Total Expenditures
Food and beverages	38.6%
Housing	10.6%
Clothing and footwear	7.2%
Transport	9.2%
Energy	5.4%
Info/communication tech	5.3%
Health	5.1%
Education	4.1%
Personal care	1.4%
Financial services	1.0%
Water and utilities	0.6%
Other	11.6%

Source: The World Bank, Share of Consumption by Sector and Consumption Segment (92 Countries), 2010

Global Advertising Expenditures

Category	2013	2014
Television	$173.31 billion	$183.50 billion
Internet	$109.69 billion	$127.35 billion
Newspaper	$76.05 billion	$73.10 billion
Radio	$30.95 billion	$31.04 billion
Outdoor	$30.62 billion	$31.75 billion
Magazines	$24.15 billion	$23.23 billion
Cinema	$2.11 billion	$2.14 billion
Total	$446.88 billion	$472.11 billion

Source: McKinsey Global Report, 2015

Advertising in the United States

Category	2014
Retail	$16.01 billion
Automotive	$15.21 billion
Telecommunications	$9.36 billion
Local services	$9.13 billion
Financial services	$7.60 billion
Personal care products	$7.03 billion
Food and candy	$6.63 billion
Restaurants	$6.45 billion
Direct response	$5.63 billion
Insurance	$5.27 billion

Source: Kantar Media

Solid Waste Disposal Methods as a Percentage of Total

Country	Landfills	Recycle	Waste-to-Energy	Other
Japan	3	17	74	6
Korea	36	49	14	—
Denmark	5.1	25.6	54.0	—
Sweden	5	34	50	1
UK	64	17	8	1
Switzerland	1	34	50	—
US	54	24	14	—
Mexico	97	3	—	—
Canada	—	26.8	—	60.7
Greece	92	8	—	—
Uganda	100	—	—	—

Source: The World Bank,
Municipal Solid Waste Disposal Methods by Country

Threats to Tropical Rainforests

Region	% Change in Rainforest Area, 2000-2005
Africa	-3.0%
Asia	+1.0%
Europe	+0.5%
Caribbean	+4.5%
Central America	-6.5%
North America	0
South America	-2.5%
Oceania	-1.0%
World	-1.0%

Source: Food and Agriculture Organization of the U.N.,
The State of the World's Forests, 2007

Causes of Tropical Deforestation

Cause	% of Total
Small-holder agriculture	35-45%
Cattle pasture	20-25%
Large-scale agriculture	15-20%
Logging	10-15%
Other	5%

Source: Mongbay.com,
Causes of Tropical Deforestation, 2000-2005

Global Greenhouse Gas Emissions by Economic Sector

Economic Sector	% of Total
Electricity and Heat Production	25%
Agriculture, Forestry, and Other Land Use	24%
Industry	21%
Transportation	14%
Buildings	6%
Other Energy	10%

Source: Intergovernmental Panel on Climate Change

Global CO$_2$ Emissions from Fossil Fuel Combustion and Some Industrial Processes

Region	% of Total
China	28%
US	16%
European Union	10%
India	6%
Russian Federation	6%
Japan	4%
Other	30%

Source: Carbon Dioxide Information Analysis Center

Organizations
to Contact

FairTrade Canada

1145 Carling Ave., Suite 7500

Ottawa, Ontario

Canada K17 7K4

Phone: 613-563-3351

Email: info@fairtrade.ca

Website: www.fairtrade.ca

Fair Trade Federation

1612 K Street, NW, Suite 600

Washington, D.C. 20006

Phone: 302-655-5203

Email: info@fairtradefederation.org

Website: www.fairtradefederation.org

The Fairtrade Foundation

3rd Floor Ibex House,

42-47 Minories

London EC3N 1DY

Phone: +44(0)203 301 5001

Email: media@fairtrade.org.uk

Website: www.fairtrade.org.uk

FairTrade International (FLO)

Bonner Talweg 177

53129 Bonn

Germany

Phone: +49-228-949230

Fax: +49-228-2421713

Email: info@fairtrade.net

Website: www.fairtrade.net

Fair Trade USA

1500 Broadway #400

Oakland, CA 94612

Phone: 510-663-5260

Fax: 510-663-5264

Website: www://fairtradeusa.org

Greenpeace USA

702 H Street, NW, Suite 300

Washington, D.C. 20001

Phone: 1-800-722-6995

Fax: (202) 462-4507

Email: info@wdc.greenpeace.org

Website: www.greenpeace.org/usa

Oxfam America

226 Causeway Street, 5th Floor

Boston, MA 02114

Phone: (800) 77-OXFAM

Website: www.oxfamamerica.org

Friends of the Earth

1101 15th Street NW, 11th Floor

Washington, D.C. 20005

Phone: 1-877-843-8687

Fax: 202-783-0444

Website: www.foe.org

World Fair Trade Organization (WFTO)

Godfried Bomansstraat 8-3

4103 WR Culemborg

The Netherlands

Phone: +31 (0) 345-53-64-87

Email: info@wfto.com

Website: www.wfto.com

World Trade Organization (WTO)

Centre William Rappard

Rue de Lausanne 154

CH-1211 Geneva 21

Switzerland

Phone: +41 (0)22 739-5111

Fax: +41 (0)22 731-4206

Email: enquiries@wto.org

Website: www.wto.org

**Organisation for Economic
Co-operation and Development (OECD)**
Washington Centre
2001 L Street, NW, Suite 650,
Washington, DC 20036-4922
Phone: (202) 785-6323
Fax: (202) 785-0350
E-mail: washington.contact@oecd.org
Website: www.oecd.org

US Chamber of Commerce
1615 H Street, NW
Washington, DC 20062
Phone: (202) 659-6000
Fax: (202) 463-3126
Email: Americas@uschamber.com
Website: www.uschamber.com

Series Glossary

apartheid—literally meaning "apartness," the political policies of the South African government from 1948 until the early 1990s designed to keep peoples segregated based on their color.

BCE and CE—alternatives to the traditional Western designation of calendar eras, which used the birth of Jesus as a dividing line. BCE stands for "Before the Common Era," and is equivalent to BC ("Before Christ"). Dates labeled CE, or "Common Era," are equivalent to *Anno Domini* (AD, or "the Year of Our Lord").

colony—a country or region ruled by another country.

democracy—a country in which the people can vote to choose those who govern them.

detention center—a place where people claiming asylum and refugee status are held while their case is investigated.

ethnic cleansing—an attempt to rid a country or region of a particular ethnic group. The term was first used to describe the attempt by Serb nationalists to rid Bosnia of Muslims.

house arrest—to be detained in your own home, rather than in prison, under the constant watch of police or other government forces, such as the army.

reformist—a person who wants to improve a country or an institution, such as the police force, by ridding it of abuses or faults.

republic—a country without a king or queen, such as the US.

United Nations—an international organization set up after the end of World War II to promote peace and co-operation throughout the world. Its predecessor was the League of Nations.

UN Security Council—the permanent committee of the United Nations that oversees its peacekeeping operations around the world.

World Bank—an international financial organization, connected to the United Nations. It is the largest source of financial aid to developing countries.

World War I—A war fought in Europe from 1914 to 1918, in which an alliance of nations that included Great Britain, France, Russia, Italy, and the United States defeated the alliance of Germany, Austria-Hungary, the Ottoman Empire, and Bulgaria.

World War II—A war fought in Europe, Africa, and Asia from 1939 to 1945, in which the Allied Powers (the United States, Great Britain, France, the Soviet Union, and China) worked together to defeat the Axis Powers (Germany, Italy, and Japan).

Further Reading

Cargill, Kima. *The Psychology of Overeating: Food and the Culture of Consumerism*. London: Bloomsbury Academic, 2015.

Dannemiller, Scott. *The Year without a Purchase: One Family's Quest to Stop Shopping and Start Connecting*. Louisville, Ky.: Westminster John Knox Press, 2015.

de Graaf, John. *Affluenza: How Overconsumption Is Killing Us—and How to Fight Back*. Oakland, Calif.: Berrett-Koehler Publishers, 2014.

Schor, Juliet B. *Born to Buy: The Commercialized Child and the New Consumer Cult*. New York: Scribner, 2014.

The Worldwatch Institute. *State of the World 2010: Transforming Cultures from Consumerism to Sustainability*. Washington, D.C.: Island Press, 2015.

Internet Resources

http://www.worldwatch.org/
Research and articles on renewable energy, nutritious food, expansion of environmentally sound jobs and development, and transformation of cultures from consumerism to sustainability.

https://en.reset.org/
News and facts about smart approaches to sustainability in climate protection, energy, city living, protecting animals, green living, and development in under-resourced countries.

https://www.oxfam.org/en
International organization that works to find practical, innovative ways for people to rise out of poverty by raising awareness, collecting data, and providing ways to take action.

http://datatopics.worldbank.org/consumption/
Global consumption database that gives consumption statistics by country, sector, or product/service.

http://web.worldbank.org
A global review of solid waste management, including information on waste collection, disposal, and effects on the environment.

http://www3.epa.gov/climatechange/

The US Environmental Protection Agency's hub for climate change, with information on greenhouse gases, statistics, and what people can do to make an impact.

http://www.mongabay.com/

Seeks to raises interest in rainforests, wild lands, and wildlife while examining the impact of emerging trends in climate, technology, economics, and finance on conservation and development.

Index

Numbers in **bold italics** refer to captions.

About the Author

Martin Johnson lives in New York City with his family. A graduate of Kings College, he is a book editor and translator. This is his first book for young adults.